THE CUTEST PUPPIES EVER!

Quarto is the authority on a wide range of topics.
Quarto educates, entertains and enriches the lives of our readers—enthusiasts and lovers of hands-on living.
www.quartoknows.com

This edition first published in 2020 by QEB Publishing, an imprint of The Quarto Group.
26391 Crown Valley Parkway, Suite 220
Mission Viejo, CA 92691, USA
T: +1 949 380 7510
F: +1 949 380 7575
www.QuartoKnows.com

Authors: Catherine Veitch & Anna Claybourne
Publisher: Maxime Boucknooghe
Designers: Mike Henson & James Handlon
Editor: Harriet Stone
Picture Researcher: Sarah Bell

A CIP record for this book is available from the Library of Congress.

ISBN 978 0 7112 5331 5

Manufactured in Guangdong, China TT102019

9 8 7 6 5 4 3 2 1

Puppy Stats contain information on color, size, and cuteness rating, plus a quick fact about each breed.

PUPPY STATS

Color: Black, brown, blue, rust

Size: Huge

They make great guard dogs.

CONTENTS

Which is the cutest of them all?
Read on and find out!

AFGHAN HOUND

This long-legged pup is built for running. Keep her on a leash when you go on walks, or she'll run off to chase small animals.

Her fur may look fluffy, but wait until your Afghan pup grows up. Her whole body will be covered in long, silky hair—even her ears and feet! Brush her every day to comb out those tangles.

PUPPY STATS

Color: Many colors
Size: Huge

An adult Afghan's hair grows down to its toes!

AKITA

Akitas love the snow. They were bred in the mountains of Japan, so don't be surprised if your Akita won't come in when he's out playing in the snow!

This feisty ball of fluff needs careful training as a puppy, so that he learns to get along with other dogs.

PUPPY STATS

Color: Many colors
Size: Huge

Akitas have webbed paws to help them walk over snow.

ALASKAN MALAMUTE

This cute, fluffy pup looks a lot like a wolf—and he *is* a lot like a wolf!

Bred for cold, snowy places, Malamutes love exercise. They need to run around outdoors, or else they'll go crazy, howl, chew up your couch, or raid the trash!

Despite all this, though, they're friendly, loyal pets.

PUPPY STATS

Color: White, shades of black
Size: Huge

Malamutes howl more than they bark.

AMERICAN BULLDOG

You can tell a Bulldog by its wide head, short muzzle, and big mouth. In puppy form, they look super-sweet.

American Bulldogs were bred to be strong, outdoor farm dogs, so they need a LOT of exercise.

Their puppies are noisy, playful, funny, and jumpy—and dribble quite a lot too! Eww!

PUPPY STATS

Color: Shades of brown, red, white, black
Size: Big

They were used to round-up hogs and cattle.

AMERICAN STAFFORDSHIRE TERRIER

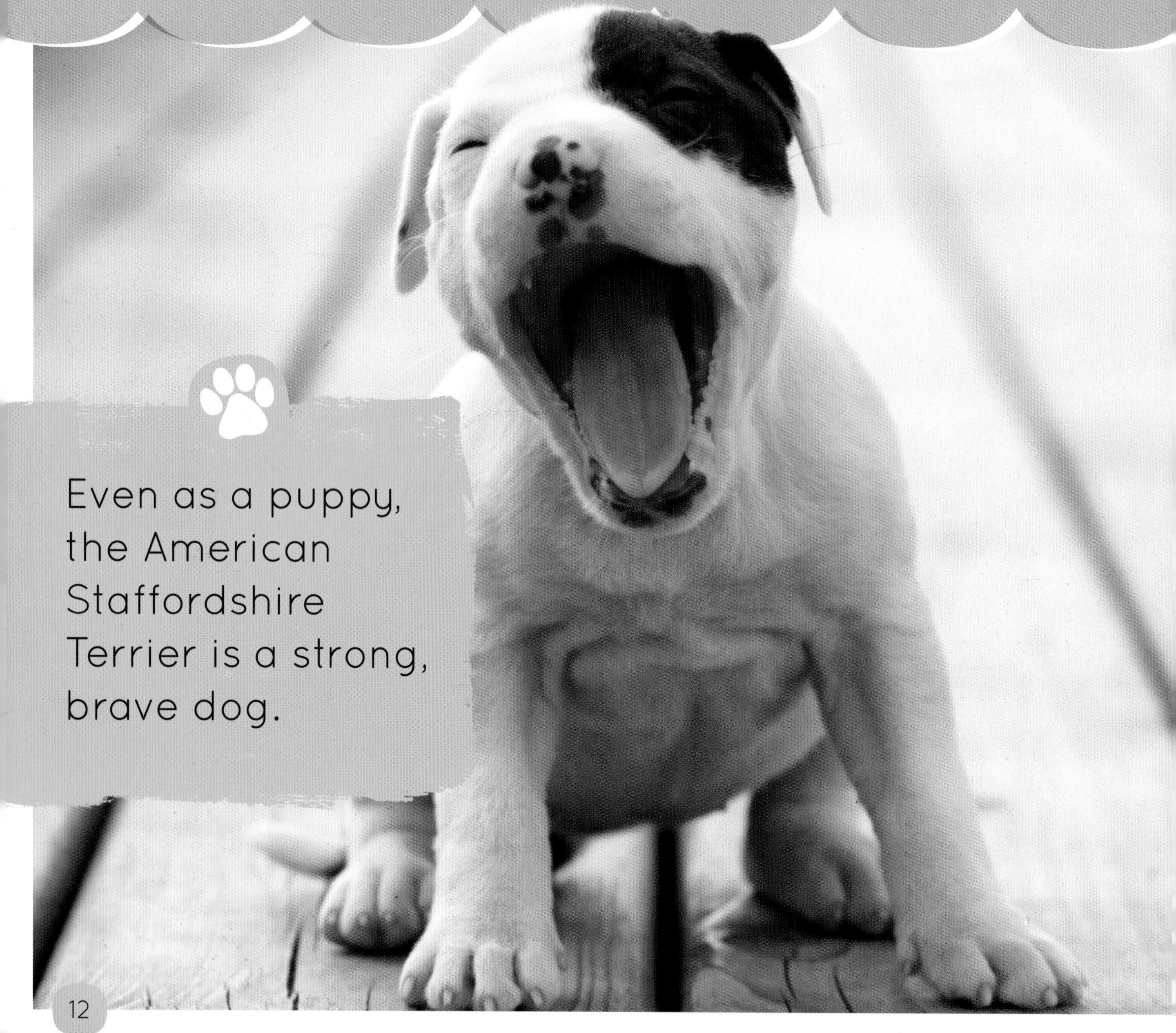

Even as a puppy, the American Staffordshire Terrier is a strong, brave dog.

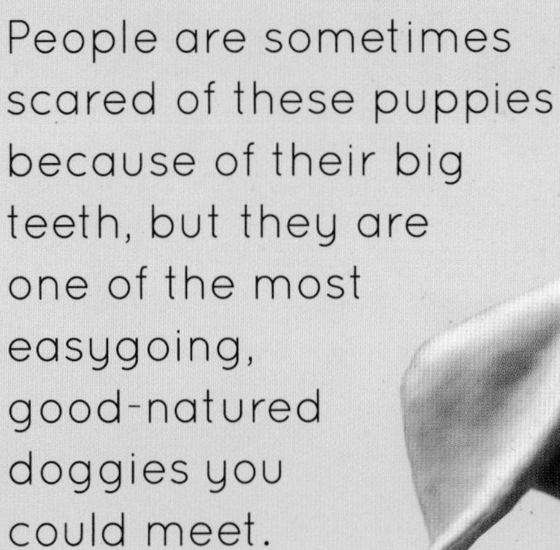

People are sometimes scared of these puppies because of their big teeth, but they are one of the most easygoing, good-natured doggies you could meet.

They'll bounce everywhere, jump up to greet you, and give you a big slobbery kiss!

PUPPY STATS

Color: White, tan, black
Size: Medium

Give your staffie pup the toughest chew toys to keep her strong jaws busy!

BASSETT HOUND

The Basset Hound is a champion sniffer and can pick up scents from a long way off. Her long, floppy ears help fan the smells to her nose.

Because your Basset pup is close to the ground she picks up dirt easily and will need lots of baths. Her big ears need cleaning once a week, too!

PUPPY STATS

Color: Many colors
Size: Small, but chunky

Basset hounds don't like swimming, so keep them away from water.

BEAGLE

Beagle puppies are a bit of a handful. They're always up to mischief—chewing things, raiding the kitchen for food, or running away to follow an interesting scent.

It's lucky they're also funny, friendly, and incredibly cute! A Beagle pup's big, brown eyes could make you forgive them for anything.

PUPPY STATS

Color: Many colors
Size: Small and squat

Known as a "nose with feet," as their nose leads the way when they pick up a scent.

BEARDED COLLIE

If you want a puppy who never stops bouncing around, a Bearded Collie is for you!

This pup gets his name from his silky-soft, waterproof coat. His endless excitement and jumpy playfulness is known as the "Beardie bounce."

He's a waggy-tailed, loyal, loving, happy-go-lucky cutie who makes a fabulously fun pet.

PUPPY STATS

Color: Black, blue, brown, fawn, white
Size: Big

They are named after the long beards they grow as adults.

BERNESE MOUNTAIN DOG

This Bernese Mountain pup may grow into a huge dog, but he'll always be a big softie.

These dogs were bred for working on farms in the Swiss mountains and need lots of exercise. They love to play the clown and make you laugh. Your pup will especially love it if you give him a job to do.

PUPPY STATS

Color: Black, rust, white
Size: Huge

The Bernese makes a good watchdog.

BICHON FRISE

Tiny, cuddly, soft, and fluffy, a Bichon Frise is the ultimate adorable pup.

He's calm, loves children, and always wants to interact.

In fact, Bichons are so sweet, caring, and sensitive, they often work as therapy dogs. They are taken into hospitals or nursing homes to snuggle with the patients and cheer them up.

PUPPY STATS

Color: White
Size: Small

The name means "curly lapdog" in French!

BORDER COLLIE

The Border Collie was bred to herd sheep, so he needs lots of space to run and play.

Watch out he doesn't try to herd the local wildlife! This pup has both brains and beauty. He's quick to learn so it's best to train him from a pup before he picks up any bad habits, like barking or nipping.

PUPPY STATS

Color: Many colors
Size: Medium

Border Collies are great at learning tricks.

BORZOI

Sweet, sensible, and laid-back—that's a Borzoi puppy. Until she sees something to chase, that is, and then zooms off at incredible speed!

In Russia, where this breed comes from, the name "Borzoi" means "fast."

Borzoi pups are also affectionate, and love to cuddle in your lap—even though they're a bit too big!

PUPPY STATS

Color: Many colors
Size: Huge

A Borzoi's nose takes three years to grow into the long nose of an adult.

CAVALIER KING CHARLES SPANIEL

Just imagine stroking this puppy's long, soft, silky ears!

Gentle and friendly, a Cavalier King Charles Spaniel puppy is the ultimate cuddly companion.

He loves curling up on your lap for some attention. But he's also a fast runner, and will chase anything—balls, cats, squirrels, even birds and butterflies!

PUPPY STATS

Color: Shades of brown, black, tan, red, white
Size: Small

They are named after a real king who took them everywhere he went!

CHIHUAHUA

This Chihuahua may be pocket-sized but she has a big personality and you will know when there's a Chihuahua around!

Chihuahuas love to burrow and will snuggle under anything including blankets, pillows, and dirty clothes. They also feel the cold so put a sweater on your pup in cold weather.

PUPPY STATS

Color: Many colors
Size: Tiny

Chihuahuas are named after the place in Mexico where they came from.

CHINESE CRESTED DOG

This funny-looking pup will melt your heart.

Chinese crested dogs are often mainly hairless, with a big fluffy "topknot" of fur on their heads.

This puppy is a loving companion. She'll climb into your bed, claim your lap as her territory, and even hug you around the neck with her paws. Awwwwww!

PUPPY STATS

Color: Many colors
Size: Small

There's no doggy smell with the hairless type, because they don't have much hair!

CHOW CHOW

Could THIS be the cutest puppy ever? With her squishy face, crumpled ears, and slightly grumpy expression, a Chow Chow puppy just makes your heart melt!

Chows are from China, where they are known as "puffy lion dogs." They have an unusual blue-black tongue, and are good at learning tricks.

PUPPY STATS

Color: Cream, gold, blue
Size: Big

They are great on a cold day as they like sitting on your feet!

COCKAPOO

A Cockapoo is a cross between a Cocker Spaniel and a Poodle. Can you guess which bits are from each dog?

This gentle, friendly, fun-loving Cockapoo just loves to spend time with you. She is a cute and cuddly fluff-ball who will make herself at home on your lap. And she's friendly with other animals, too!

PUPPY STATS

Color: Many colors
Size: From small to big

Often used as therapy dogs for people in hospitals and nursing homes.

CORGI

With his short, stubby legs, eager face, and fluffy fur, a Corgi pup is like a real live plush doggy toy!

Corgis aren't just cute though—they are reliable, brave dogs who like to guard their family home.

They love children, but watch out: a Corgi pup can sometimes be naughty and give you a nip!

PUPPY STATS

Color: Light brown, red, black, white
Size: Medium

Corgis are a favorite with the British queen!

DACHSHUND

This cutie is also known as a doxie or a sausage dog.

Dachshunds LOVE to eat, so be careful you don't overfeed your little pup, however cute he looks!

These are loyal dogs and will bond closely to one person. They like to have all of your attention and may bark at unexpected visitors.

PUPPY STATS

Color: Many colors
Size: From miniature to small

Dachshunds live for a long time. One lived for a record-breaking 21 years!

DALMATIAN

Famous for his gorgeous spotted coat, this is a puppy with a BIG personality.

Dalmatian pups have endless high-speed energy, and the waggiest tails ever! They just love to leap all over you, and they adore children and families.

They're bouncy, energetic, and sometimes a bit of a handful!

PUPPY STATS

Color: White with black or brown spots

Size: Big

Puppies are born white and don't get spots until about four weeks old.

DOBERMAN PINSCHER

Look at this puppy's alert, intelligent eyes!

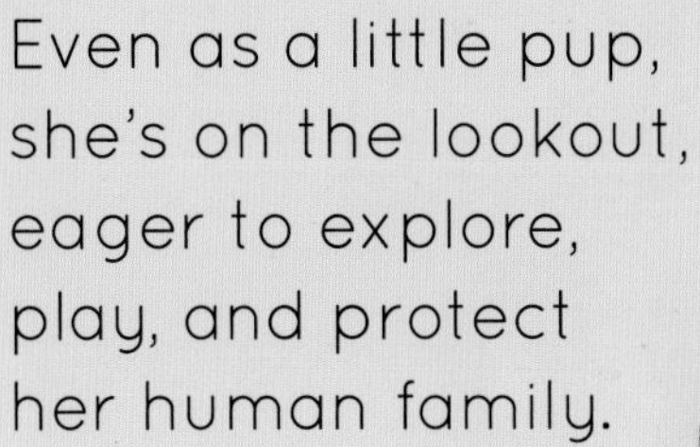

Even as a little pup, she's on the lookout, eager to explore, play, and protect her human family.

Doberman Pinschers learn easily, and can become brilliant guard dogs or police dogs. But they're not as scary as some people think—they're just big softies who are fiercely loyal!

PUPPY STATS

Color: Black, brown, blue, rust
Size: Huge

They make great guard dogs.

GERMAN SHEPHERD

So sweet and fluffy, this gorgeous puppy will grow into a confident, brave, and devoted dog.

The German Shepherd is one of the most popular pet dogs of all. These pups love to run, jump, fetch, and play.

They're smart and make great police dogs, guard dogs, guide dogs, or rescue dogs.

PUPPY STATS

Color: Black, light brown, white
Size: Huge

Those goofy, floppy ears will stand upright when they're grown up.

This Golden Retriever pup is like a snuggly, cuddly, cute little teddy bear!

These doggies make great family pets. They're sweet, friendly, happy, tail-waggy bundles of joy, who love to play with and please their owners.

Even when they grow up, they keep their puppy attitude—bouncy, silly, and fun!

PUPPY STATS

Color: Shades of gold or white
Size: Big

These sweet-natured pets make great guide dogs.

GREAT DANE

Dogs don't come much bigger than a Great Dane. Even as a puppy, he's a giant with a loud bark.

These pups can be clumsy and messy. They will knock over and squash most of the stuff in your house as they leap around wagging their tails!

But underneath, they are gentle, easygoing, and loving.

PUPPY STATS

Color: Fawn, blue, black, white
Size: Huge

The tallest dog ever was a Great Dane named Zeus who was 44 inches tall.

GREYHOUND

Greyhounds are FAST runners. Even the puppies have long legs, sleek bodies, and love chasing anything they can.

Once they've had a good run, Greyhound pups are calm, sweet, and gentle.

A Greyhound's short hair means it can get chilly. So if it's cold, get your Greyhound pup a cozy coat!

PUPPY STATS

Color: Many colors
Size: Big

Most Greyhounds like to lie down rather than sit because of how their bodies are made.

HAVANESE

With his soft silky coat, bright eyes, and floppy ears, a Havanese is just so lovable!

Small, snuggly, and cuddly, this puppy needs to be close to people. Don't leave him alone for long—he'll miss you too much! Awwww!

Havanese pups are also playful, curious, smart, and great at learning tricks.

PUPPY STATS

Color: Many colors
Size: Tiny

These small dogs can be trained for big jobs like being service dogs for the deaf.

IRISH SETTER

An Irish Setter puppy is the comedy clown of the dog world. She's excitable, silly, nosy, and full of love and affection.

She's also adorable to stroke and cuddle, with her silky soft fur and floppy ears. Though a jumpy and excitable puppy, she'll grow up to become a proud, brave, and loyal pet.

PUPPY STATS

Color: Chestnut red, with some white

Size: Big

They love to join their owners on a run or a bike ride.

IRISH WOLFHOUND

An Irish Wolfhound puppy is a big, lovable buffoon with a funny face and incredibly cute, pleading eyes.

These sweet, gentle dogs have very long legs, and as puppies, they're often adorably clumsy and goofy. They also need lots of strokes and hugs.

They don't make good guard dogs though—they're too soft!

PUPPY STATS

Color: Many colors
Size: Huge

They can grow to seven feet tall standing on their back legs!

JACK RUSSELL

Life will never be dull with a Jack Russell around! These chatty little dogs are bundles of energy.

Jack Russells were bred as working dogs and like to be kept busy. They need entertaining all the time, so be ready to join in with the fun from digging and jumping, to chasing things and exploring.

PUPPY STATS

Color: Mainly white, with black or tan

Size: Small

Jack Russells are super-bouncy and can leap five times their own height!

KOMONDOR

Where am I!? With a straggly, wooly coat that often grows over his eyes, a cute Komondor puppy looks like a hyperactive mop running around on four legs.

But this shaggy Hungarian breed is tougher than he looks.

He'll grow into a big and strong (but still very mop-like!) guard dog, who's fiercely protective of his family.

PUPPY STATS

Color: White, some cream, light brown
Size: Huge

This sheepdog's white coat meant it was well hidden among the sheep it watched!

LABRADOR RETRIEVER

The Labrador Retriever is a friendly, playful breed—and as a bouncy, cuddly puppy, she's even more fun!

Labrador puppies just love rolling around, play-fighting, and chasing things. They have warm, open faces and big, adoring eyes.

Labradors were bred to retrieve (fetch) things from water, so they like getting wet, too.

PUPPY STATS

Color: All colors
Size: Extra large

These dogs were used to hunt wild boar and deer.

MINIATURE SCHNAUZER

What could be more adorable than a tiny puppy with a big beard and mustache!?

Miniature Schnauzers are friendly, feisty puppies with a serious fluffiness factor. They're always over the moon to see you, and will make you laugh by chasing things and trying to get your attention.

PUPPY STATS

Color: White, black, silver
Size: Tiny

A little dog with a big voice!

NEWFOUNDLAND

Newfoundland dogs are big—VERY big! So a Newfie puppy can cause chaos as she bounces and leaps around. CRASH!

However, these pups make great pets, as they are kind, sweet-natured, and gentle.

Newfoundlands were bred to help fishermen in the water, so they LOVE swimming—and even have webbed toes!

PUPPY STATS

Color: Black, brown, gray, white
Size: Huge

Nana in the Peter Pan story was a Newfoundland.

OLD ENGLISH SHEEPDOG

Look at this pup's face—sweet, gentle, and just a bit mischievous!

Old English Sheepdog puppies are energetic and need exercise and space. They'll leap all over you, drool, get covered in twigs, and track mud across the floor.

To make up for it, they're big, friendly softies who'll be loyal to you forever.

PUPPY STATS

Color: Shades of gray, blue, and white

Size: Big

Be ready for a lifetime of grooming with this fluffy pup!

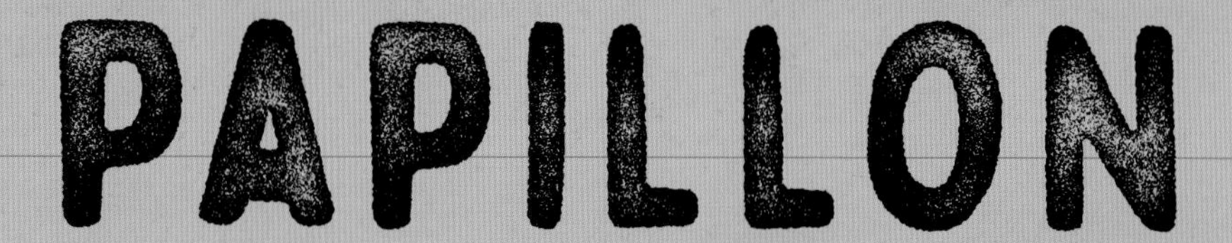

PAPILLON

This breed is named the "Papillon," meaning butterfly, thanks to its big, beautiful, butterfly-shaped ears.

Papillon puppies are bright and friendly. They are fast learners, and love playing games with their owners.

They're so small, sweet, and well-behaved, this is the kind of pup you might see a movie star carrying in her handbag!

PUPPY STATS

Color: Black, brown, white
Size: Tiny

Watch your puppy's silky hair grow as it gets older, especially on its ears.

POMERANIAN

These adorable little puffballs are also named "poms" or "pom poms."

Don't let their cuteness fool you, as poms have minds of their own! You may hear a Pomeranian before you see her as she loves to bark. Teach her when she's a pup so she learns when to be quiet.

PUPPY STATS

Color: Many colors
Size: Tiny

Many Pomeranian puppies change color as they grow up!

POODLE

People often think of Poodles as fluffy, pretty, and cute, with their soft curly coats and sweet eyes. And they certainly are!

But a Poodle pup is no slouch. These puppies are great at running, jumping, and leaping around obstacle courses.

They're also super-smart, and love to interact, play, and learn new tricks.

PUPPY STATS

Color: Many colors
Size: From tiny to medium

A Poodle's fur never stops growing, so it needs trips to the groomer often!

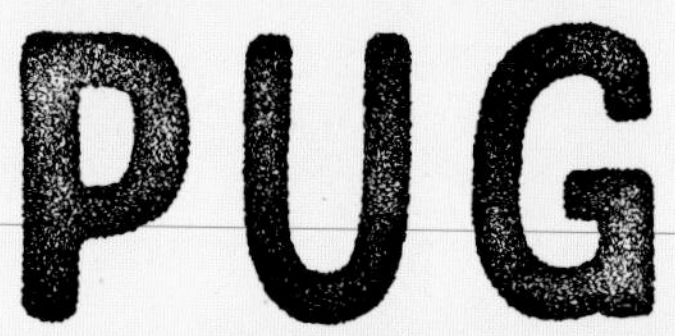

PUG

It's no surprise that this wrinkly-faced pup's favorite place is right by your side, because pugs were bred in China as lapdogs for royalty.

Pugs love snoozing and snoring indoors. But they like to go out for short walks, too, when it's not too hot or too cold.

PUPPY STATS

Color: Fawn, black, silver
Size: Tiny

A group of pugs is called a "grumble!"

PULI

This tangled ball of wooly tassels has springs hidden in her feet!

Puli pups are amazingly acrobatic and wonderful at jumping. They are also curious, playful, mischievous, and bossy, and will try to trick humans into doing what they want.

Own a Puli, and she'll wrap you around her little paw!

PUPPY STATS

Color: White, gray, black, light brown

Size: Small

The Puli likes to exercise her mind with some brain games.

RHODESIAN RIDGEBACK

These are lovable dogs who will protect the whole family.

Rhodesian Ridgebacks, or "ridgies," were bred as hunting dogs and love chasing things, so keep your gentle giant on a leash on walks.

They also love their food and will gobble up your dinner, even if they have just eaten their own!

PUPPY STATS

Color: Tan to reddish-gold, with some black
Size: Huge

The name comes from a ridge of fur that grows along its back.

ROTTWEILER

A Rottweiler is a big, strong, loud dog, and as a puppy he's full of energy and excitement.

He's always jumping up, slobbering, and romping around, and will chase cats and smaller dogs if he gets a chance.

With training, though, he'll grow into a loyal, loving pet who adores his family.

PUPPY STATS

Color: Black, brown
Size: Huge

Loves swimming, walking, and trotting alongside its owner.

SHAR-PEI

As soon as you see this bundle of wrinkly fur, you just want to stroke and snuggle him!

The Chinese Shar-Pei is prized for his unusual looks—baggy skin, tiny ears, a curly tail, and a big head that's said to look like a hippo's! They make calm, loving, chilled-out puppies.

PUPPY STATS

Color: Many colors
Size: Medium

They have a lavendar or a blue-black tongue!

SHIH TZU

The Shih Tzu was bred to be a cuddly companion, and her impossibly cute face would make anyone want to stroke and pet her.

Her name means "lion dog," but she's not fierce at all! This happy, bright-eyed puppy only wants to make friends, lie on laps, or snuggle up in a cozy bed.

PUPPY STATS

Color: Many colors
Size: Tiny

Trim the hair on its head or tie in a top knot to keep it out of its eyes.

VIZSLA

You can see in this puppy's big, wise eyes just how smart and thoughtful he is.

A Vizsla pup is quick to learn, with a great sense of smell—they often become working sniffer dogs. What they want most is to be around people, and to be stroked, petted, and loved. Awww!

PUPPY STATS

Color: Shades of gold
Size: Big

Like to exercise their minds and bodies.

WEIMARANER

With their sleek gray coats and gorgeous blue or golden eyes, Weimaraners are beautiful puppies.

But beware—they're into everything! They'll chew up your shoes, chase cats, and destroy whole couches.

They'll also follow you around like a shadow, as they can't get enough of being walked, stroked, and hugged!

PUPPY STATS

Color: Shades of gray
Size: Big

Newborn puppies have light blue eyes and dark gray stripes.

YORKSHIRE TERRIER

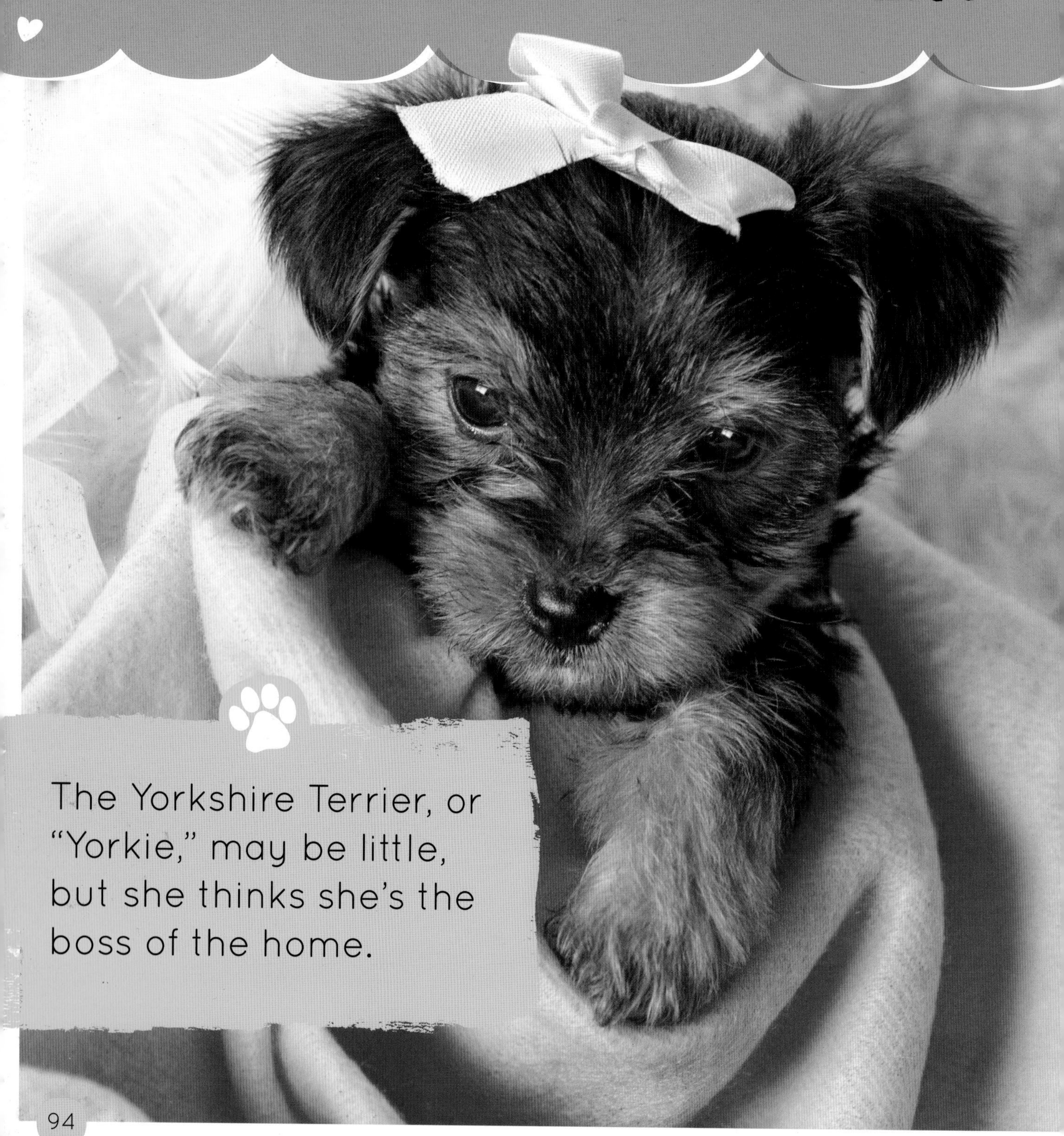

The Yorkshire Terrier, or "Yorkie," may be little, but she thinks she's the boss of the home.

She is as confident, energetic, and brave as pups many times her size. Your pup has super-hearing, too and can hear your visitors before they even ring the doorbell.

PUPPY STATS

Color: Blue, tan, black, gold
Size: Tiny

If a Yorkie's hair isn't cut it will keep on growing, just like our hair!

PICTURE ACKNOWLEDGMENTS

Back cover OlesyaNickolaeva / shutterstock.com; front cover Dmitry Kalinovsky / shutterstock.com; Alamy 17; alekuwka 79 centre; alternate take photography AU 53; Ammit Jack 85 centre; Andraz Cerar 22; Aneta Jungerova 13 below centre; anetapics 17 below; Anke Van Wyk 31 centre; Anna Mandrikyan/ Shutterstock.com 63; Anna Utekhina 62; bingdian/Getty Images 76; Bob and Pam Langrish KA9Photo / Alamy Stock Photo 35; Canon Boy 13; Cheryl E. Davis 94; Chris Lofty / Alamy Stock Photo 89; Christopher Howey 16; Cris Kelly 45 centre; Dehlodi1 93 centre; Dora Zett 23, 43 left; Eduardo Lomonaco/Getty Images 54; Evan Meyer 71 centre; Evgeniy Zakharov 25 left; Farlap / Alamy Stock Photo 14, 15; Farlap 9; Fedora_M 61 centre; Fotyma 1, 29; Getty Images Kerstin Meyer 69; Grossemy 7 left; GROSSEMY VANESSA / Alamy Stock Photo 34, 52 Guy J. Sagi 50; H. Mark Weidman Photography / Alamy Stock Photo 68; Hans Surfer/Getty Images 55 centre; Hugo Felix 47 centre; igartist 53 centre; Ilona Nagy/Getty Images 81; ImageBROKER 64; imageBROKER/ Ariane Lohmar 78; imageBROKER/Alessandra Sarti 93; Ivaylo Sarayski / Alamy Stock Photo 77; Jarry 32, 33 left; Jessica Lynn Culver/Getty Images 91; Jill Lehmann Photography/Getty Images 21; JLSnader 84; Jonathan Brizendine 29 left; JStaley401 69 left; Julija Sapic 87 centre; Juniors Bildarchiv GmbH / Alamy Stock Photo 80; Juniors Bildarchiv GmbH 59; Kate Grishakova/Shutterstock.com 70; Kelley Stanley/ Stockimo 42; Kimberly Madson 37 centre; kirendia 37; knape/Getty Images 31; Kseniya Ragozina 63 centre; KUNIAKI OKADA/ amanaimagesRF/Getty Images 27; Lenkadan 33; Little Moon 11; Lunja87 81 centre; Lurin 46; MaraZe 66, 67 centre; Mark McElroy 21 centre; Marta Pospisilova 24; Mdorottya 55; Mikkel Bigandt 49 centre, 72; Mila Atkovska 65 left; MIXA 39; Morten Normann Almeland 95; nancy dressel 83; Natalia Fedosova/Shutterstock.com 74; Nico Muller Art 57 centre, 95 left; Oleksiy Rezin, Shutterstock.com 2; Onetouchspark 4, 5, 5 centre; otsphoto 83 centre; otsphoto/Shutterstock.com 20; Paul Park/Getty Images 38; PCHT 77 centre; Phase4Studios/Shutterstock.com 8; PHOTOCREO/Michal Bednarek 27 left; Photowitch 23 centre; PozitivStudija 44, 45; Rabyesang 88 centre; Ravi Kumar / EyeEm/Getty Images 60; REX Shutterstock imageBROKER 43; Rita Kochmarjova 39 left, 47, 75, 85; Robynrg 15 left; Saranya Loi 88; Sergey Bogdanov 9 left; Sergey Lavrentev 12, 73, 73 centre, 74 left; Shutterstock.com 49, 65; sima 7; spartasibe 79; stahkmedia 36; Stephanie Frey 67; Steve Pepple 30; Suwat wongkham/Shutterstock.com 35 centre; Tierfotoagentur/Ivonne Felgenhauer 41; Tierfotoagentur/J. Hutfluss 56; Tierfotoagentur/Jeanette Hutfluss 41 centre; Tierfotoagentur/K. Luehrs 28; Tierfotoagentur / Alamy Stock Photo 10; Tierfotoagentur/R. Richter 11 left; Tkatsai 82; TongRo Images / Alamy Stock Photo 71; Trybex 6; Vanessa Grossemy 18, 86; Viorel Sima/ Shutterstock.com 96; Vivienstock 51 centre; VJDora/Getty Images 91 centre; Vudhikrai/Shutterstock.com 48; Wavetop 57; Wild Horse Photography 25; WILDLIFE GmbH / Alamy Stock Photo 59 right; WILDLIFE GmbH 92; Xalanx 40; Zoonar GmbH / Alamy Stock Photo 51; Zuzana BuráĐová / Alamy Stock Photo 87; Zuzana Tillerova 19 centre, 61; Zuzana Uhlikova 26; Zuzule 19, 58, 90